SPORTING SPACES

VOLUME 2

SPORTING SPACES

VOLUME 2

A PICTORIAL REVIEW

First published in Australia in 2003 by
The Images Publishing Group Pty Ltd
ABN 89 059 734 431
6 Bastow Place, Mulgrave, Victoria, 3170, Australia
Telephone: +61 3 9561 5544 Facsimile: +61 3 9561 4860
Email: books@images.com.au
Website: www.imagespublishinggroup.com

The Images Publishing Group Reference Number: 400

National Library of Australia Cataloguing-in-Publication data

Sporting spaces: a pictorial review

Includes index.
ISBN: 1 86470 034 3 (v.2)

1. Stadiums—design and construction. 2. Recreation centers—design and construction.
3. Sports facilities—design and construction.

725.8043

Co-ordinating Editor: Sarah Noal
Designed by The Graphic Image Studio Pty Ltd, Mulgrave, Australia
Film by Mission Productions Limited
Printed by Everbest Printing Co. Ltd. in Hong Kong/China

IMAGES has included on its website a page for special notices in relation to this and our other publications. Please visit this site: www.imagespublishinggroup.com

CONTENTS

Asian Games Aquatic Centre
Bangkok, Thailand
Cox Richardson

1 Aquatic Centre from plaza
2 Aquatic Centre plaza entry
3 Competition pool

Photo credit: Graham Sands

1

2

3

4

5

Asian Games Aquatic Centre
Bangkok, Thailand
Cox Richardson
4&5 Diving pool and competition pool
Photo credit: Graham Sands

Twinsburg High School Fitness Center
Twinsburg, Ohio, USA
Fanning/Howey Associates, Inc.

1 Serpentine glass-block wall separates fitness center from natatorium
2 Entrance
3 Reception area
4 Natatorium is used for competitive and recreational purposes

Photo credit: Emery Photography, Inc.

1

2

3

4

adidas

2

3

Athletes' Performance Institute
Tempe, Arizona, USA
GouldEvans

Opposite:
Six 12-foot-high (3.7-meter-high) overhead glass sectional doors open for training flexibility

2 Entry lobby flooded with natural light

3 Cantilevered wall animates hallway with layering of natural light, athletic memorabilia, and color

Following pages:
Transparent north façade at dawn

Photo credit: Bill Timmerman

Athletes' Performance Institute
Tempe, Arizona, USA
GouldEvans

Opposite:
View through steel stair to athlete lounge beyond and mezzanine above

6 Open-web steel structure facilitates 70-foot (21-meter) clear-span in athlete training area

7 Clean lines frame building entry

8 Structural steel frame is simultaneously exposed and concealed

Photo credit: Bill Timmerman

6

7

8

Victorian Gymnastics and National Institute of Circus Arts, Prahran Campus, Swinburne University of Technology Melbourne, Victoria, Australia
Bates Smart

1 Principal elevation, Green Street
2 Rhythmic gymnastics studio, men's gymnastics to right, NICA studio to left
3 Northwest elevation with roof access and escape stair
4 NICA training studio
5 NICA training studio, rhythmic gymnastics studio to left

Photo credit: Chris Atkins

1

2

3

4

5

Victorian Gymnastics and National Institute of Circus Arts, Prahran Campus, Swinburne University of Technology, Melbourne, Victoria, Australia
Bates Smart

6 NICA training studio looking toward rhythmic gymnastics studio

7 NICA training studio, rhythmic gymnastics studio to left

Photo credit: Chris Atkins

6

7

University of the Sunshine Coast Recreation Club
Sippy Downs, Queensland, Australia
Architectus Sydney, designers Kerry and Lindsay Clare (Adjunct Professors of the University of Sydney, Faculty of Architecture)

1 Looking southeast with amenities pavilion to right
2 Looking south along west veranda
3 Northwest corner showing light, shade and ventilation strategies of multi-layered roof
4 Looking north in class/clubroom
5 Bar/servery at south end of main room

Photo credit: Richard Stringer

1

2

3

4

5

1

Atago Green Hills
Tokyo, Japan
Cesar Pelli & Associates in association with Jun Mitsui & Associates

1 Spa's pool on 42nd floor
2 Aquarium with optical fiber natural lighting system in spa corridor
3 Spa's bathroom on 42nd floor
4 Spa's gym on 42nd floor

Photo credit: Kawasumi Architectural Photograph Office

2

3

4

Atago Green Hills
Tokyo, Japan
Cesar Pelli & Associates in association with Jun Mitsui & Associates

Opposite:
Spa's elevator hall
6 Spa's dressing room
7 Spa's curved wall
Following pages:
Night view of spa's pool

Photo credit: Kawasumi Architectural Photograph Office

6

7

1

2

Lane Cove Aquatic Leisure Centre
Lane Cove, New South Wales, Australia
Michael Davies Associates Pty Ltd, Architects

1 25-meter pool looking south
2 25-meter pool
3 Free-form leisure pool
4 Spa pool and pamper area
5 Building entry by night
6 Pool hall looking over 25-meter pool

Photo credit: Brett Boardman

3

4

5

6

C. Bernard Shea Rowing Center
Princeton, New Jersey, USA
ARC/Architectural Resources Cambridge, Inc.

1 New addition
2 View from Washington Street Bridge
3 Corridor featuring photos of past crews
4 16-person rowing tank
5 Training room with exposed timber trusses

Photo credit: Nick Wheeler/Wheeler Photographics

1

2

3

4

5

C. Bernard Shea Rowing Center
Princeton, New Jersey, USA
ARC/Architectural Resources Cambridge, Inc.

6 Training room with ergometers
7 Renovated tower that serves as new main entrance
8 Trophy case in refurbished clubroom
9 Tower interior featuring donor plaques

Photo credit: Nick Wheeler/Wheeler Photographics

6

7

8

9

1

Bad Elster Spa
Bad Elster, Germany
Behnisch & Partner

1 Leafed glazing filters light and color onto neutral surfaces
2 Outdoor pool
3 Old forms contrast with new
4 Glass is white frit-printed on upper sides and color frit-printed on lower sides

Photo credit: Christian Kandzia

2

3

4

Bad Elster Spa
Bad Elster, Germany
Behnisch & Partner

5 Lockers bring color inside
6 Louvers regulate light and temperature for bathers' comfort
7 Steel-grid structure supports louver system above pools
8 Courtyard baths were added to historic spa

Photo credit: Christian Kandzia

GSP Stadium and Athletic Centre
Nicosia, Republic of Cyprus
Theo. David Architects—TDA/KAL

9 Berm detail
10 South entrance elevation
11 Spiral spectator ramp view
12 Overall view of main football stadium pitch
13 Entrance detail

Photo credit: Theo. David

5

6

7

8

9

10

11

12

13

1

2

Chesterton High School
Chesterton, Indiana, USA
Fanning/Howey Associates, Inc.

1 Main entrance of new 515,000-square-foot (47,850-square-meter) building
2 Chesterton High School main lobby
3 Aerobic and dance studio
4 22,000-square-foot (2044-square-meter) eight-lane competition natatorium

Photo credit: Emery Photography, Inc.

3

4

Chesterton High School
Chesterton, Indiana, USA
Fanning/Howey Associates, Inc.

5 Sports training/clinic and student instructional space
6 17,057-square-foot (1585-square-meter) spectator gym seats 4181
7 Weight and fitness rooms
8 33,500-square-foot (3112-square-meter) fieldhouse with indoor running track

Photo credit: Emery Photography, Inc.

UQ Centre, the University of Queensland
Brisbane, Queensland, Australia
PDT Architects

9 Main 3 court hall
10 Main entrance to UQ Centre
11 External view

Photo credit: courtesy the University of Queensland

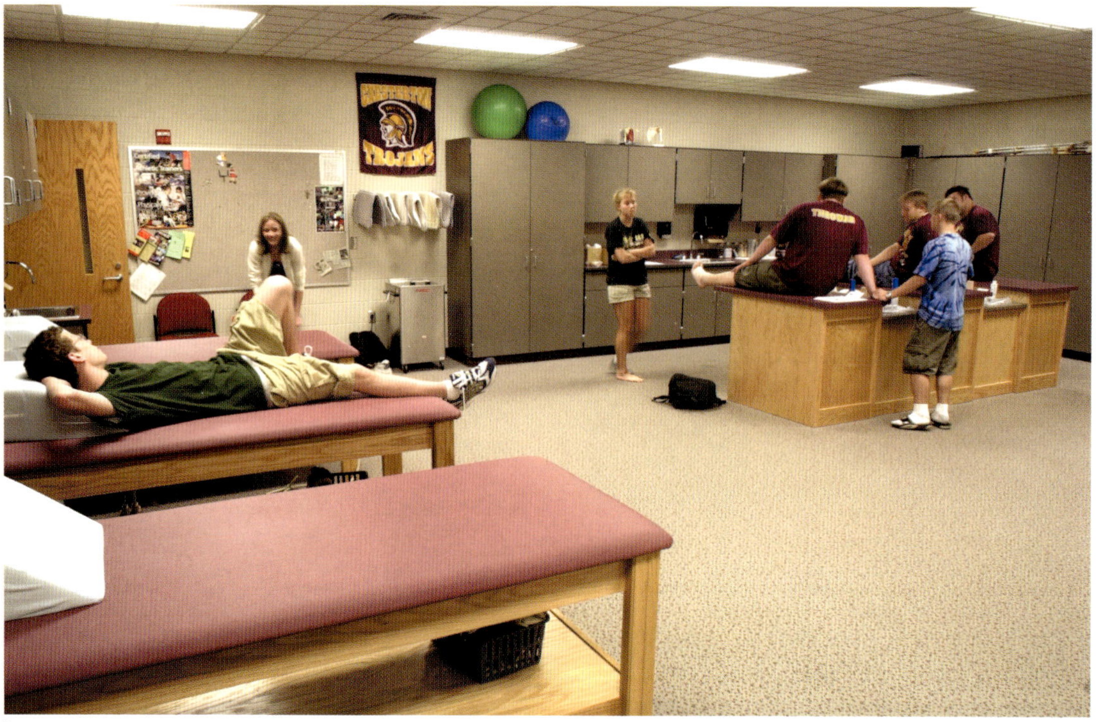

5

6

7

8

9

10

11

1

Asian Games Athletic Centre
Bangkok, Thailand
Cox Richardson

1 Aerial view
2 Dragon entrance sculpture

Photo credit: Graham Sands

2

Asian Games Athletic Centre
Bangkok, Thailand
Cox Richardson

3 Stadium lighting mast
4 Stadium arena
5 Axial approach to stadium

Photo credit: Graham Sands

3

4

5

6

7

Asian Games Athletic Centre
Bangkok, Thailand
Cox Richardson

6 Landscaped terraces at stadium approach
7 Stadium by night
8 Stadium roof

Photo credit: Graham Sands

8

1

2

3

Republic of Singapore Yacht Club
Singapore, Republic of Singapore
Alfred Wong Partnership Pte Ltd

1 Tensile canopy over dining terrace
2 View of F&B facilities on ground floor and second floor, and close-up view of swimming pool
3 View of entire complex with clubhouse facilities to right and hotel wing to left
4 View from second-floor lobby overlooking swimming pool terrace

Photo credit: Albert Lam AMPA

4

5

6

7

Republic of Singapore Yacht Club
Singapore, Republic of Singapore
Alfred Wong Partnership Pte Ltd

5 Night view of main clubhouse
6 View from upper colonnade toward swimming pool deck and marina
7 View of main clubhouse showing clubhouse facilities and outdoor seating and swimming pool
8 View from viewing terrace toward marina

Photo credit: Albert Lam AMPA

8

1

2

Conseco Fieldhouse
Indianapolis, Indiana, USA
Ellerbe Becket

1 Conseco Fieldhouse, home of the NBA Indiana Pacers
2 Sports bar on main concourse
3 Entry pavilion
4 One of Conseco Fieldhouse's retro-themed concourses

Photo credit: Timothy Hursley

HOME OF THE
CONSECO FIELDHOUSE
INDIANA PACERS
MARSH
3

Talk of Indiana
TELEPHONE
PACERS BANKING
One at a time please!
Entry Pavilion
a True Pilsner.
CLOSED
CLOSED
4

2

3

Oakland University Student Recreation and Athletic Center
Rochester, Michigan, USA
Cannon Design in association with TMP Associates

Opposite:
Racquetball courts
2 Exercise fitness room
3 50-meter pool area includes spectator seating for 1000

Following pages:
Student recreation integrated with facilities for competitive athletics

Photo credit: Greg Hursley

East Hampton RECenter
East Hampton, New York, USA
Davis Brody Bond

1 View of exterior looking north
2 Twilight view through to interior multipurpose space
3 Detail of cedar wood sun shading on south façade
4 Pedestrian bridge between facilities
5 View of exterior cedar shiplap siding and sunshades

Photo credit: Paul Warchol

1

2

3

4

5

6

7

8

9

East Hampton RECenter
East Hampton, New York, USA
Davis Brody Bond

6 Ramp dividing atrium's lounge and fitness areas

7 View of instructional pool

8 View of lap and secondary pools looking north

9 Lounge and fitness areas beneath skylight

Photo credit: Paul Warchol (6,7,9); David Sunberg/Esto (8)

Ski 'n' Skurf Cable Ski Park
Bli Bli, Queensland, Australia
Architectus Sydney, Designers Kerry and Lindsay Clare (Adjunct Professors of the University of Sydney, Faculty of Architecture)

10 East façade overlooks lake and 'skurf' cable system

11 Ancillary spaces grouped around main roof

12 Detail of northeast entry veranda

13 Timber entry ramp at lake's edge

14 View over 'skurf' launch pad

Photo credit: Adrian Boddy

10

11

12

13

14

Hong Kong Institute of Education,
Pak Shek Kok Sports Centre
Hong Kong SAR, PRC
P&T Group

1 Site plan
2 Track
3 Stadium
4 View from stadium to 400-meter athletic track

Photo credit: P&T Photographic Department

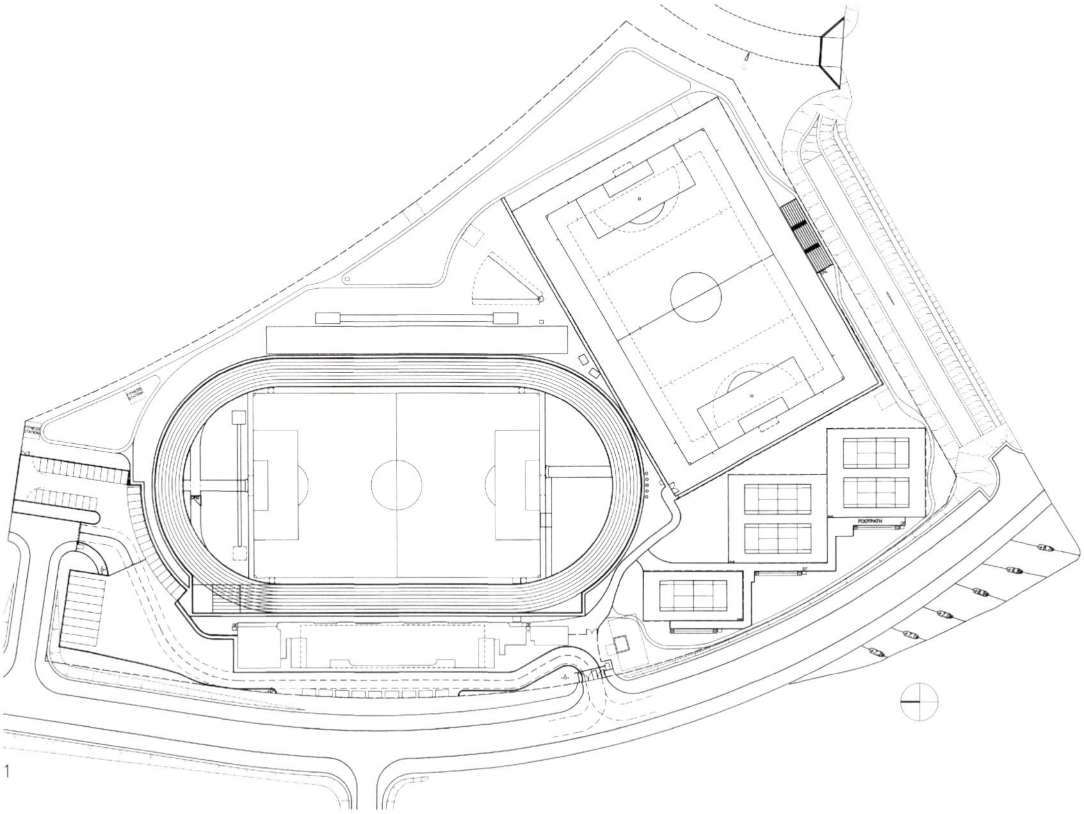

1

2

3

4

Hong Kong Institute of Education, Pak Shek Kok Sports Centre
Hong Kong SAR, PRC
P&T Group

5 View of stadium seats
6 View of 30-meter lighting masts
7 View of track

Photo credit: P&T Photographic Department

The Cauldron, Overflow Park
Homebush Bay, New South Wales, Australia
Alexander Tzannes Associates

8 Olympic cauldron
9 Underside of cauldron
10 Name plates and child running through fountain

Photo credit: Bart Maiorana

University of Newcastle Sports, Health and Recreation Building
Newcastle, New South Wales, Australia
Group GSA

11 Competition basketball court
12 Indoor rock-climbing facilities
13 Olympic-standard 50-meter indoor swimming pool

Photo credit: Andrew Payne

5

6

7

8

9

10

11

12

13

The NovaCare Complex: Training Facility for the Philadelphia Eagles
Philadelphia, Pennsylvania, USA
Michael Graves & Associates

1 Entrance from parking lot into two-story Eagles' wing
2 Dining terrace overlooking playing field

Opposite:
Players' locker room

Photo credit: Matt Wargo

1

2

4

The NovaCare Complex: Training Facility for the Philadelphia Eagles
Philadelphia, Pennsylvania, USA
Michael Graves & Associates
4 Entrance lobby for Eagles' headquarters
5 Executive waiting area
6 189-seat auditorium
Following pages:
Weight room
Photo credit: Matt Wargo

5

6

AVENGER
AVENGER
AVENGER
PULLDOWN
AVENGER
YORK

1

2

3

4

Sports Center, National Taiwan University
Taipei, Taiwan
Haigo Shen & Partners

1 View from northeast
2 Close view from northeast
3 Interior view of main arena
4 Aerial view from northeast

Photo credit: Jeffrey Cheng

1

2

3

4

5

Sydney International Regatta Centre
Penrith Lakes, New South Wales, Australia
Woods Bagot
1 Boatshed and pavilion at dusk
2 View toward course
3 Terraced spectator stand holds up to 1000 people
4 Light steel frame structure uses environmentally friendly materials
5 Regatta Centre hosted 2000 Olympic rowing, sprint and slalom canoe/kayak events
6 Aerial view of Regatta Centre site
Photo credit: Patrick Bingham-Hall

Asian Games Gymnasium 3
Rangsit, Bangkok, Thailand
SJA 3D Co., Ltd.
7 Front elevation on north side
8 Indoor stadium of 387,000 square foot (36,000 square meters) with total capacity of 8000 seats
9 Interior of main entrance lobby
Photo credit: courtesy SJA 3D Co., Ltd.

6

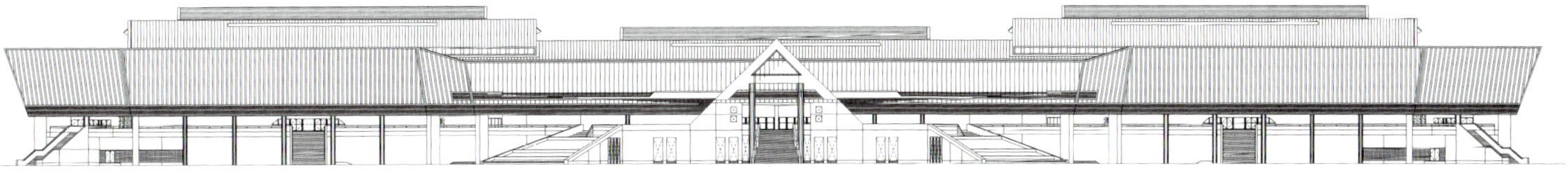

7

8

9

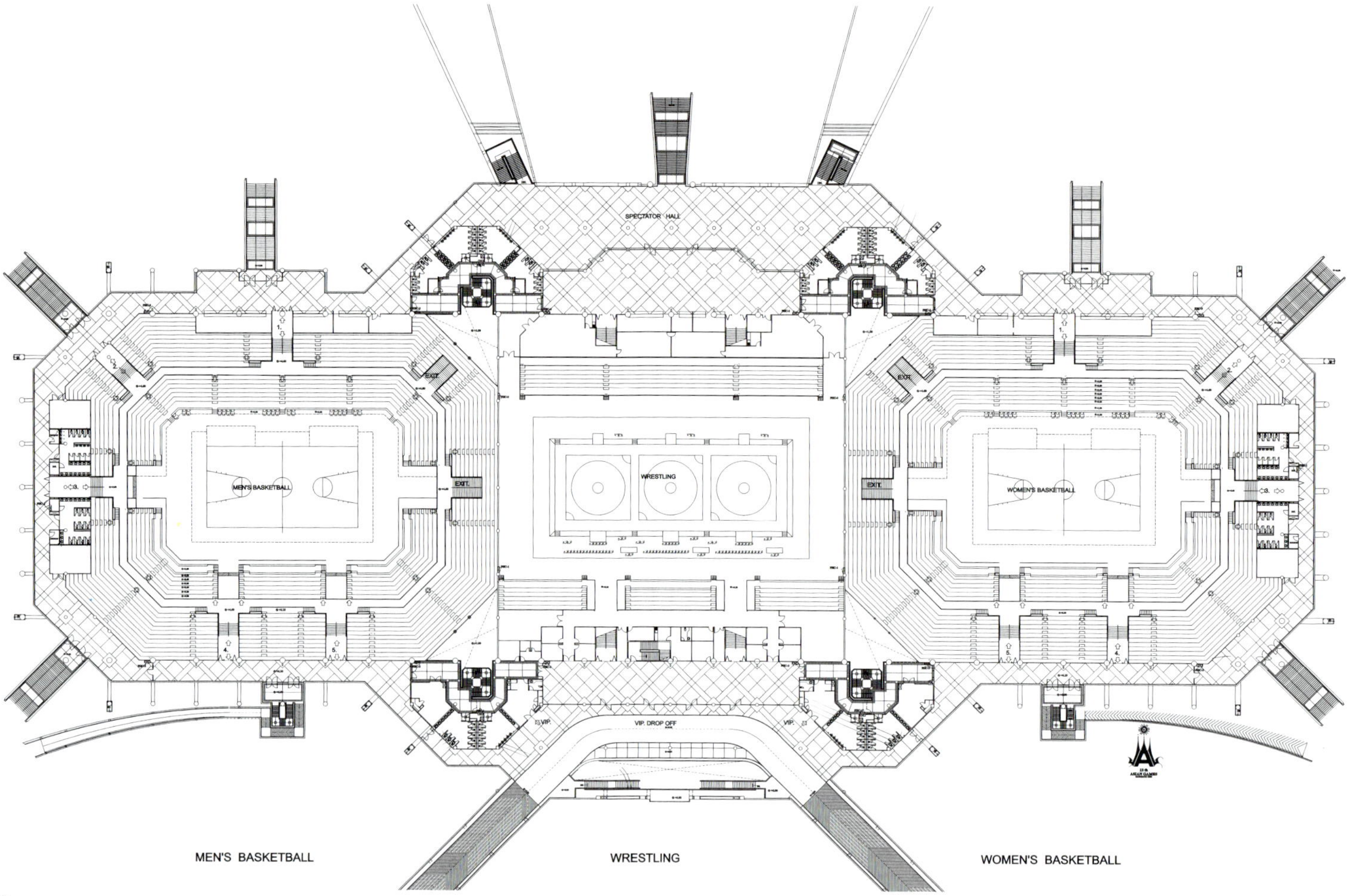

10

11

12

13

14

15

16

Asian Games Gymnasium 3
Rangsit, Bangkok, Thailand
SJA 3D Co., Ltd.

10 General plan of indoor sports facilities
11 View of basketball court
12 Portico at main entrance lobby

Photo credit: courtesy SJA 3D Co., Ltd.

Diversey Driving Range
Diversey Parkway and Lake Shore Drive, Chicago, Illinois USA
DeStefano + Partners, Ltd

13 South elevation from main entry stair
14 View from west
15 Detail of second-level balustrade
16 South elevation looking west

Photo credit: Barbara Karant

Suncorp Metway Stadium at Lang Park
Brisbane, Queensland, Australia
PDT Architects in association with HOK Sport + Venue + Event

17 Aerial montage perspective, looking west showing north and south plaza, Hale Street plaza, and main stadium
18 Aerial montage perspective, looking east toward Brisbane central business district
19 View over pitch from television interview studio

Photo credit: courtesy HOK Sport + Venue + Event and PDT Architects in association

17

18

19

1

MG MOBILE GLASS
employment NATIONAL
City of Joondalup
Bakers Delight
Honeywell
AMP
PRIME realty
KFC

2

3

4

5

Joondalup Aquatic Centre
Perth, Western Australia, Australia
Cox Howlett & Bailey Woodland

1 View from north
2 Competition pool
3 Leisure pool
4 Lazy River ride
5 Learn-to-swim pool

Following pages:
Joondalup Stadium from football field

Photo credit: Graham Sands

Coca-Cola
BAR

BAR

1

3

2

Cawthra Community Center
Mississauga, Ontario, Canada
Diamond and Schmitt Architects Incorporated

1 Entry gallery, upper level
2 Entry gallery, main level
3 Gymnasium—composite timber and steel trusses, and full-height glazing

Photo credit: Steven Evans

4

Cawthra Community Center
Mississauga, Ontario, Canada
Diamond and Schmitt Architects Incorporated

4 Gymnasium—upper level walking track with perforated steel guard panels
5 Active living studio—sprung wood floor for aerobics, ballet and yoga
6 Gymnasium—composite timber and steel trusses, and full-height glazing

Photo credit: Steven Evans

University of Tasmania Martial Arts Dojo
Hobart, Tasmania, Australia
Jacob Allom Wade Architects

7 Dojo entry walk provides contemplative separation from outside world
8 University of Tasmania Martial Arts Dojo
9&10 Environment to encourage harmony, vitality, discipline, coordination, and contemplation

Photo credit: David Button

5

6

7

CHILDCARE
CENTRE
USERS ONLY
¼P
→ University Community
Child Care Centre
8

9

10

Guangdong Olympic Stadium
Guangzhou, PRC
Ellerbe Becket
1 Processional stadium entrance, 100-room hotel to right
Photo credit: Ou, Xiaomin

1

2

3

Guangdong Olympic Stadium
Guangzhou, PRC
Ellerbe Becket

2 Opening ceremonies, Chinese National Games

3 Seating bowl looking toward end-zone area

4 Exterior view of Guangdong Olympic Stadium

Photo credit: Ou, Xiaomin

4

Sydney International Shooting Centre
Sydney, New South Wales, Australia
Group GSA

1&2 10-, 25-, and 50-meter and finals ranges accommodating different shooting disciplines

3 Designed and built for Sydney 2000 Olympic Games in environmentally sensitive rural area

Following pages:
Designed using recycled timber in compliance with environmentally sustainable design principles

Photo credit: Patrick Bingham-Hall

1

2

3

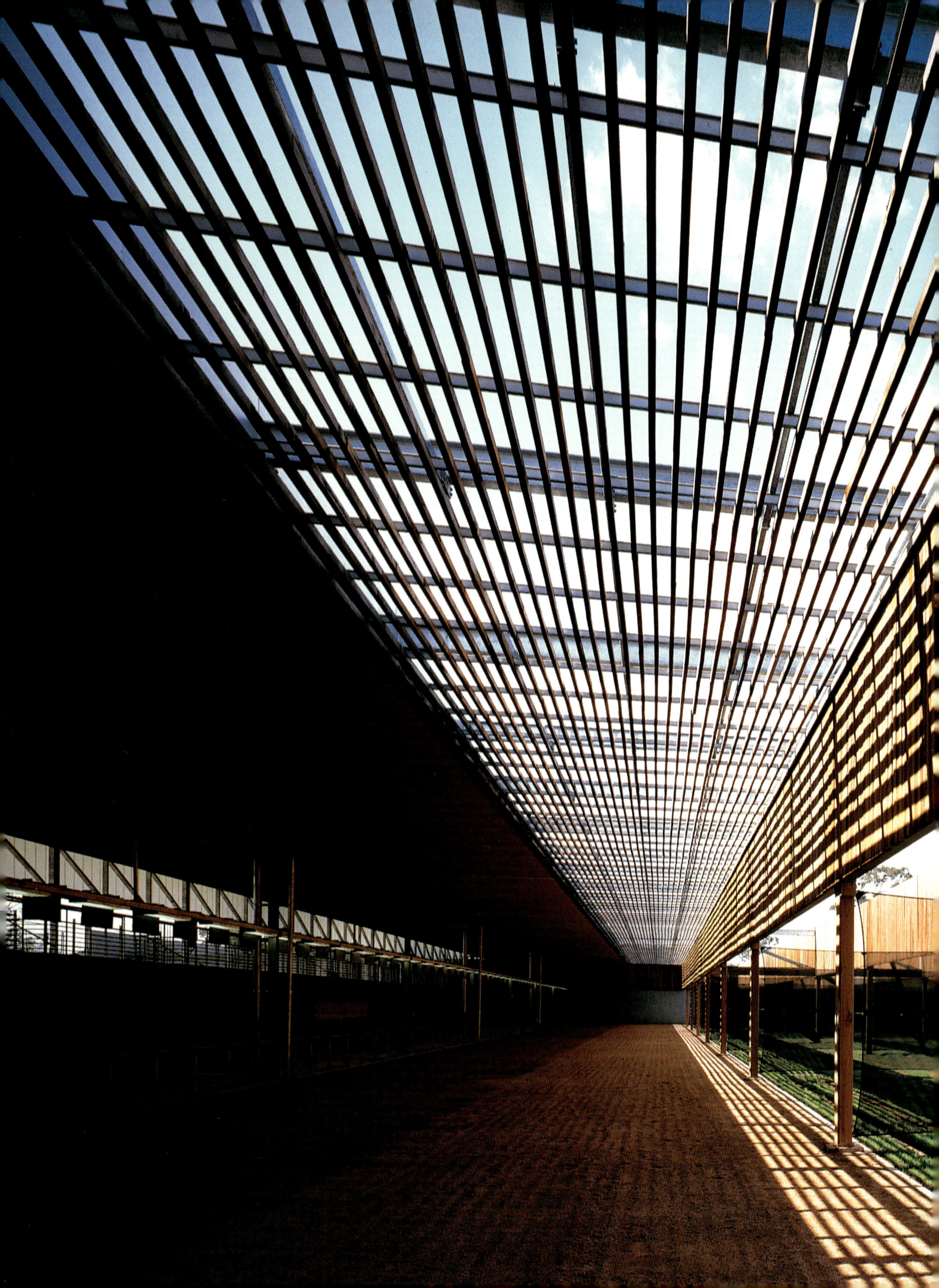

The Venue
Borehamwood, Hertsmere, UK
FaulknerBrowns Architects

1 Main entrance and Churchillian colonnade
2 Entrance at night
3 Front elevation
4 Entrance elevation
5 Pool hall with teaching pool and gym

Photo credit: Ian Lawson

1

2

3

4

5

The Venue
Borehamwood, Hertsmere, UK
FaulknerBrowns Architects

6 Precast concrete Churchillian columns to front elevation
7 Competition pool hall
8 View from health suite into pool
9 Main entrance and column
10 Main entrance
11 Entrance to gym on first floor

Photo credit: Ian Lawson

6

7

8

9

10

11

1

2

Superdome
Homebush Bay, New South Wales, Australia
Cox Richardson

1 Arena
2 View from main concourse
3 View from northern arrival
4 Foyer

Following pages:
View from main concourse

Photo credit: Patrick Bingham-Hall

3

4

SONY SuperDome
Tickets

1

Asphalt Green AquaCenter
New York, New York, USA
Richard Dattner & Partners Architects

1 Concrete waves greet swimmers and visitors
2 Waving façade softens building's impact on adjoining park
3 AquaCenter wedged between highway, ramp and playground

Photo credit:Jeff Goldberg/ESTO

2

3

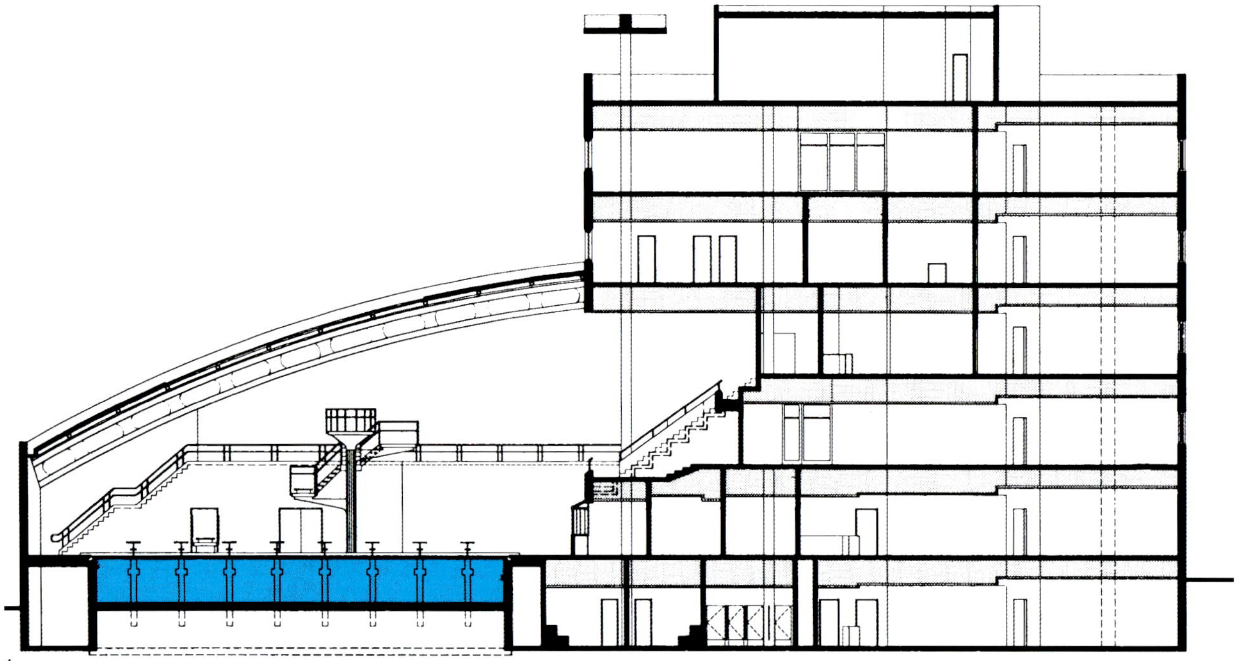

4

5

Asphalt Green AquaCenter
New York, New York, USA
Richard Dattner & Partners Architects

4 Section through pool and activity floors
5 South wall facing playing field
6 Curved steel trusses enclose pool

Photo credit: Jeff Goldberg/ESTO

6

7

Asphalt Green AquaCenter
New York, New York, USA
Richard Dattner & Partners Architects

7 Asphalt Plant and AquaCenter along FDR Drive

Photo credit:Jeff Goldberg/ESTO

1

4

2

5

3

6

7

8

9

Mingara Leisure Centre
Central Coast, New South Wales, Australia
Woods Bagot

1 Fun pool
2 Lap pool
3 Night view of entrance
4 Outdoor entertainment area
5 Mingara Leisure Centre services Central Coast area of New South Wales

Photo credit: Christopher Shain

University of Illinois at Chicago
Chicago, Illinois, USA
SmithGroup JJR

6 Soccer field (action)
7 Softball field
8 Volleyball courts and concession
9 Athletic complex (aerial)

Photo credit: courtesy SmithGroup JJR

Rough Creek Lodge
Glen Rose, Texas, USA
Lawrence W. Speck of
PageSoutherlandPage

1 Terraces from main lodge step to lake
2 Lodge is wrapped around some of ranch's largest live oak trees

Opposite:
Entrance to hunters' quarters frames view of lake

Photo credit: Greg Hursley

1

2

5

6

7

Rough Creek Lodge
Glen Rose, Texas, USA
Lawrence W. Speck of PageSoutherlandPage

Opposite:
Ruggedness of natural landscape is matched in building façades

5 Hunting atmosphere permeates interior

6 Fireplace is centerpiece of main lodge room

7 Stone piers give building feeling of heft and permanence

Following pages:
Exterior circulation keeps hunters connected with outdoors

Photo credit: Greg Hursley

Saitama Super Arena
Saitama, Japan
Ellerbe Becket

1 Entrance plaza
2 Seating bowl and event floor
3 Seating bowl view from courtside restaurant
4 Exterior

Photo credit: Kokyu Miwa Architectural Photography Laboratory

1

2

3

4

1

2

3

4

5

6

7

8

9

Swimming Pool Complex
Leipzig, Germany
Behnisch, Behnisch & Partner

1 Wing slabs overlap for dynamic structure
2 Glass blurs inside/outside boundary
3 View to pool
4 Tiled shower
5 Swim hall
6 Café
7 Slide

Photo credit: Christian Kandzia

Hindmarsh Soccer Stadium
Adelaide, South Australia, Australia
Woods Bagot

8 Grandstand seating—spectator view
9 Hindmarsh was redeveloped to FIFA requirements

Photo credit: Aspect Photographics

Hindmarsh Soccer Stadium
Adelaide, South Australia, Australia
Woods Bagot

10 Home to Sydney 2000 Olympics Soccer
11 Hindmarsh Stadium in action
12 External grandstand façade and graphics
13 External grandstand detail
14 Entrance to stadium at night
15 Inside grandstand

Photo credit: Aspect Photographics

10

11

12

13

14

15

16

17

18

Casey Aquatic Centre
Casey, Victoria, Australia
Cox Sanderson Ness

16 Main pool
17 Casey Aquatic Centre at dusk
18 Leisure pool

Photo credit: Dianna Snape

Mitchell Field Community Centre
North York, Ontario, Canada
Kuwabara Payne McKenna Blumberg Architects

1 East–west cross section
2 North–south cross section
3 Center combines warm palette of materials with striking color elements

Opposite:
Spacious multipurpose gymnasium with mezzanine running track

Photo credit: Michael Awad

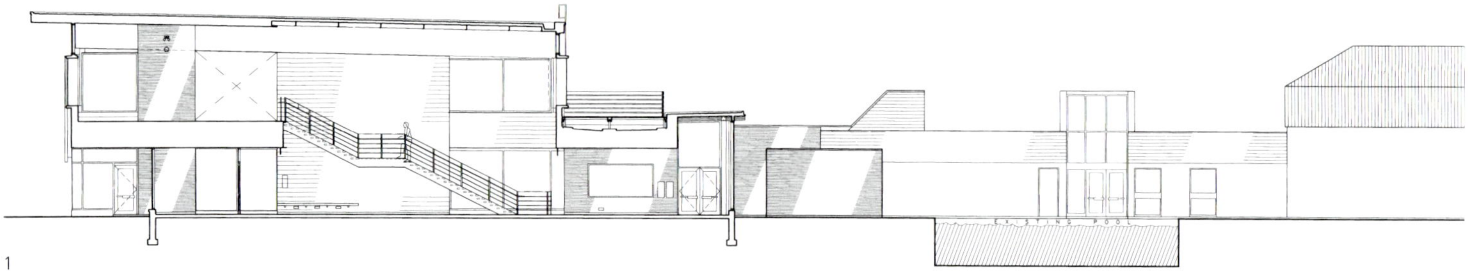

1

2

3

EXIT

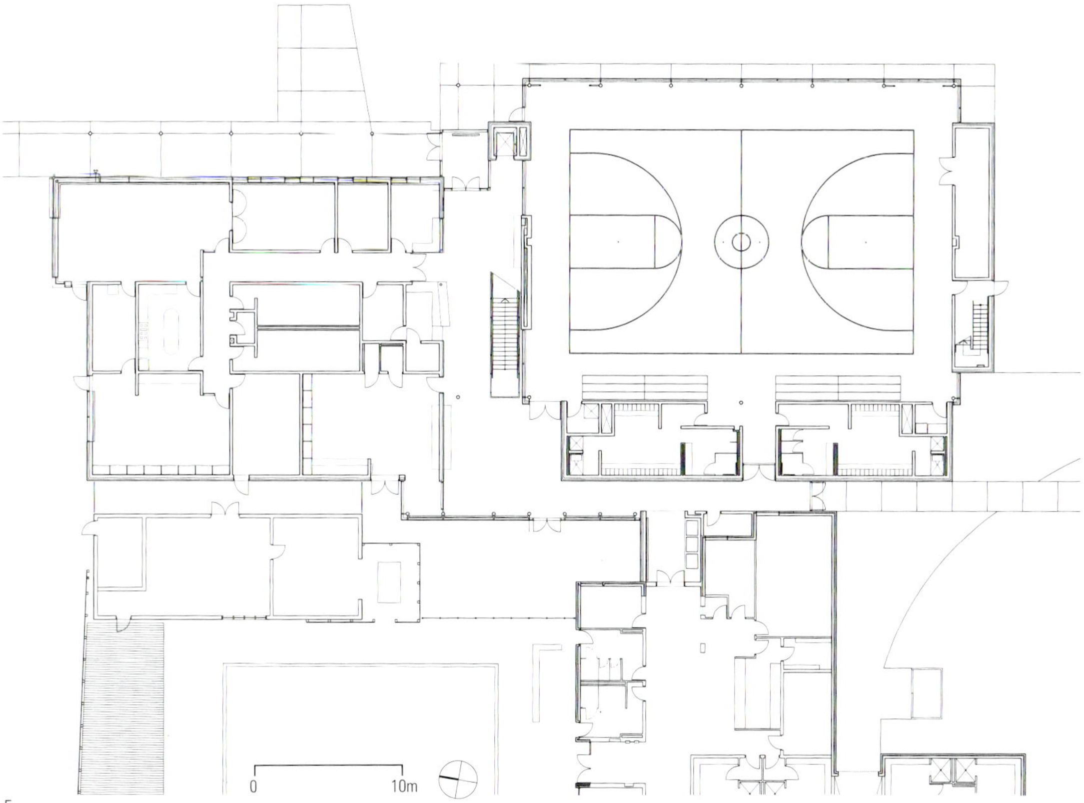

5

Mitchell Field Community Centre
North York, Ontario, Canada
Kuwabara Payne McKenna Blumberg Architects

Opposite:
View of public foyer and stair to track level

5 Ground floor plan

6 View of sheltered walkway to main entrance

Photo credit: Michael Awad

6

1

2

3

4

5

6

7

Texas A&M Sports & Recreation Building
College Station, Texas, USA
Marmon Mok

1 10-meter and springboard diving platforms as seen from spectator viewing area
2 Building entrance, north elevation; weight room and archery to left, natatorium to right
3 Main east–west corridor dividing gymnasium racquetball area from public entrance and rock-climbing wall to left
4 50-meter competition pool, seen from dive pool
5 Indoor quarter-mile running track overlooking indoor soccer/basketball court

Photo credit: John Dyer (1); Greg Hursley (2–4); Aker/Zvonkovic (5)

Guangzhou Gymnasium
Guangzhou, PRC
Paul Andreu Architecte/ADPi

6 Main covered stadium
7–9 Exterior view

Photo credit: Juillet 2001 © Li Wen/Point Studio

8

9

Victorian Racing Club Members' Grandstand, Flemington Racecourse
Flemington, Victoria, Australia
The Buchan Group

1 Open terraces
2 Grandstand is used as a venue for functions on non-race days
3 Interior spaces and glazing allow patrons to mingle away from viewing seats but still enjoy trackside action

Following pages:
New grandstand sits above former Prince of Wales stand and between Hill stand and old Member's grandstand

Photo credit: Tim Griffith

2

1

3

Victorian Racing Club Members' Grandstand, Flemington Racecourse
Flemington, Victoria, Australia
The Buchan Group

5 Forum Bar on level one, with overhead electronic display of racing information

6 Chairman's Club on level three has a restaurant, cinema-quality viewing seats, lounges, bar, and wagering facility.

7 Grandstand's unique curving profile—an icon for Flemington Racecourse

Photo credit: Tim Griffith

5

6

7

Riverbank State Park
New York, New York, USA
Richard Dattner & Partners Architects

1 Illuminated skylights invite visitors to park
2 Riverbank resembles aircraft carrier in Hudson River

Opposite:
Park entrance, skating rink and cultural center

Photo credit: Norman McGrath

1

2

Riverbank State Pa

4

5

6

Riverbank State Park
New York, New York, USA
Richard Dattner & Partners Architects

4 Gymnasium accommodates variety of activities

5 Entrance lobby to interior recreation facilities

6 50-meter pool, divisible into three zones

Photo credit: Norman McGrath (4,5); Stanley Greenberg (6)

Manuka Oval Redevelopment
Canberra, Australian Capital Territory, Australia
Woods Bagot
1 External façade
Photo credit: Tim Linkins

1

2

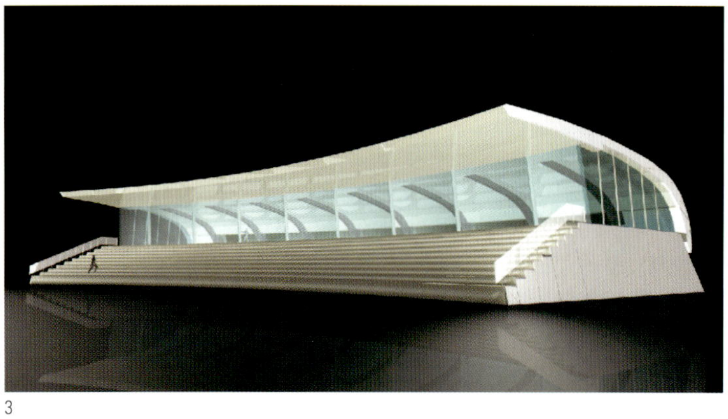
3

4

Manuka Oval Redevelopment
Canberra, Australian Capital Territory, Australia
Woods Bagot

2 New covered grandstand holds up to 10,000 people
3 Three-dimensional rendering of front of stadium
4 Corporate entertainment areas

Photo credit: Tim Linkins

Kilpatrick Athletic Center, Simon's Rock College of Bard
Great Barrington, Massachusetts, USA
Centerbrook Architects and Planners

1 Site for Athletic Center is main gateway to campus
2 Entrance
3 Juice bar in lobby
4 Basketball court and running track
5 Upper lobby

Photo credit: Steve Rosenthal

1

2

3

4

5

Kilpatrick Athletic Center, Simon's Rock College of Bard
Great Barrington, Massachusetts, USA
Centerbrook Architects and Planners

Opposite:
Climbing wall
7 Squash courts

Photo credit: Steve Rosenthal

7

8

9

10

11

12

Kilpatrick Athletic Center, Simon's Rock College of Bard
Great Barrington, Massachusetts, USA
Centerbrook Architects and Planners

8 Pool washed in diffused natural light to avoid glare that could distract athletes
9 Fitness center
10 Pool has southern yellow pine laminated trusses that create soaring space

Photo credit: Steve Rosenthal

University of Minnesota Football Complex (Hall of Fame and Weight Training Gym)
Minneapolis, Minnesota, USA
Ellerbe Becket

11 Entry to Hall of Traditions
12 Exhibit floor

Photo credit: Dana Wheelock

13

14

University of Minnesota Football Complex (Hall of Fame and Weight Training Gym)
Minneapolis, Minnesota, USA
Ellerbe Becket

13 Exhibit display
14&15 Strength and conditioning gymnasium

Photo credit: Dana Wheelock

15

Gymnasium and Indoor Swimming Pool, Chung-Yuan Christian University Chungli, Taiwan

J.J. Pan and Partners, Architects and Planners in association with C.H. Wang, Architect

1 Main court
2 Front entrance of swimming pool
3 Upper lobby
4 Gymnasium lobby

Following pages:
Swimming pool interior

Photo credit: Bor-Nian Lin (1,Following pages); Gina Lin (2,3,4)

1

2

3

4

8
7

1

2

3

4

KidsPeace Aquatic Center
Orefield, Pennsylvania, USA
Spillman Farmer Architects

1 Operable skylights bring the outdoors in but keep the elements out

Photo credit: Steven Wolf Photography

Goodwill Games Swimming and Diving Complex
East Meadow, New York, USA
Richard Dattner & Partners Architects

2 Landscaped berm leads to spectator entrance

3 Concrete diving platform support echoes buttresses

4 Masonry base with pool-level entrance

Photo credit: Peter Mauss/Esto

5

Goodwill Games Swimming and Diving Complex
East Meadow, New York, USA
Richard Dattner & Partners Architects

5 View of pool, diving platforms, central skylight

6 Tensile fabric overhang controls sunlight

Photo credit: Peter Mauss/Esto

6

1

2

Kooyong Lawn Tennis Club
Melbourne, Victoria, Australia
Six Degrees Architects
1–3 West façade
4 Court side
5 Glazing detail—Aztec Glass
Photo credit: John Gollings

3

4

5

6

7

Kooyong Lawn Tennis Club
Melbourne, Victoria, Australia
Six Degrees Architects

6 Indoor swimming pool
7 Dining room
8 Gymnasium

Following pages:
West view of tennis courts from clubhouse

Photo credit: John Gollings

8

'yes'

Irwin Indoor Practice Facility,
University of Illinois
Champaign, Illinois, USA
RATIO Architects

1 Elevation view looking east
2 Practice field interior
3 View looking southwest
4 North entry portal
5 Practice field interior

Photo credit: © Bob Haar/Hedrich Blessing

1

2

3

4

5

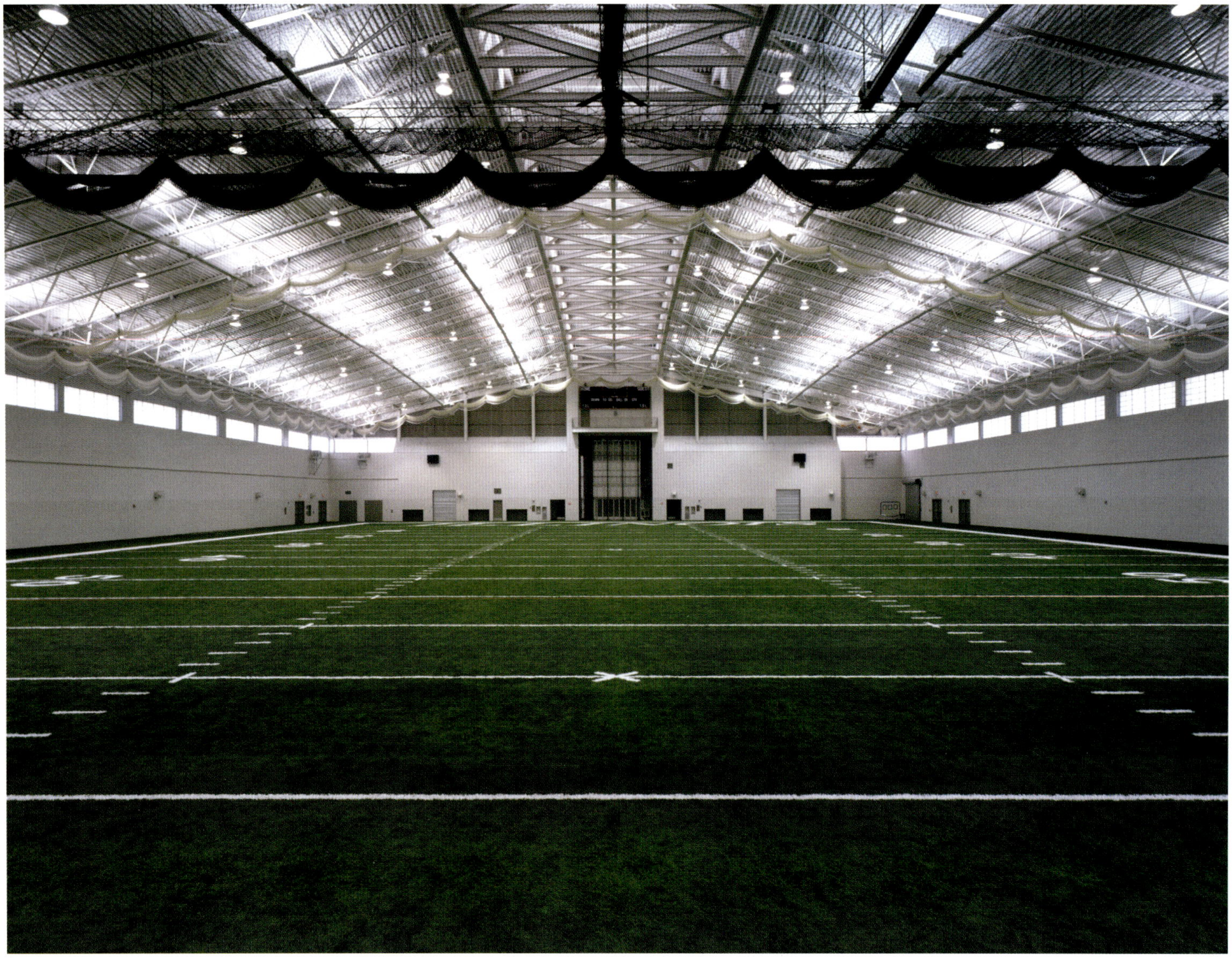

6

7

8

Irwin Indoor Practice Facility,
University of Illinois
Champaign, Illinois, USA
RATIO Architects

6 Practice field interior

Photo credit: © Bob Haar/Hedrich Blessing

James W. Garrett Sports and Fitness Complex, Susquehanna University
Selinsgrove, Pennsylvania, USA
Spillman Farmer Architects

7 Glass wall at night

8 51,000-square-foot (4738-square-meter) field house

Opposite:
Indoor six-lane 200-meter track

Photo credit: Steven Wolf Photography

1

2

Lance Armstrong Recreation Center,
Nike World Campus
Beaverton, Oregon, USA
Thompson Vaivoda & Associates Architects, Inc.

1 One of three sand volleyball courts on building's south side
2 Looking south across soccer fields to Lance Armstrong Building
3 Primary building entry, north elevation

Photo credit: Strode Photographic

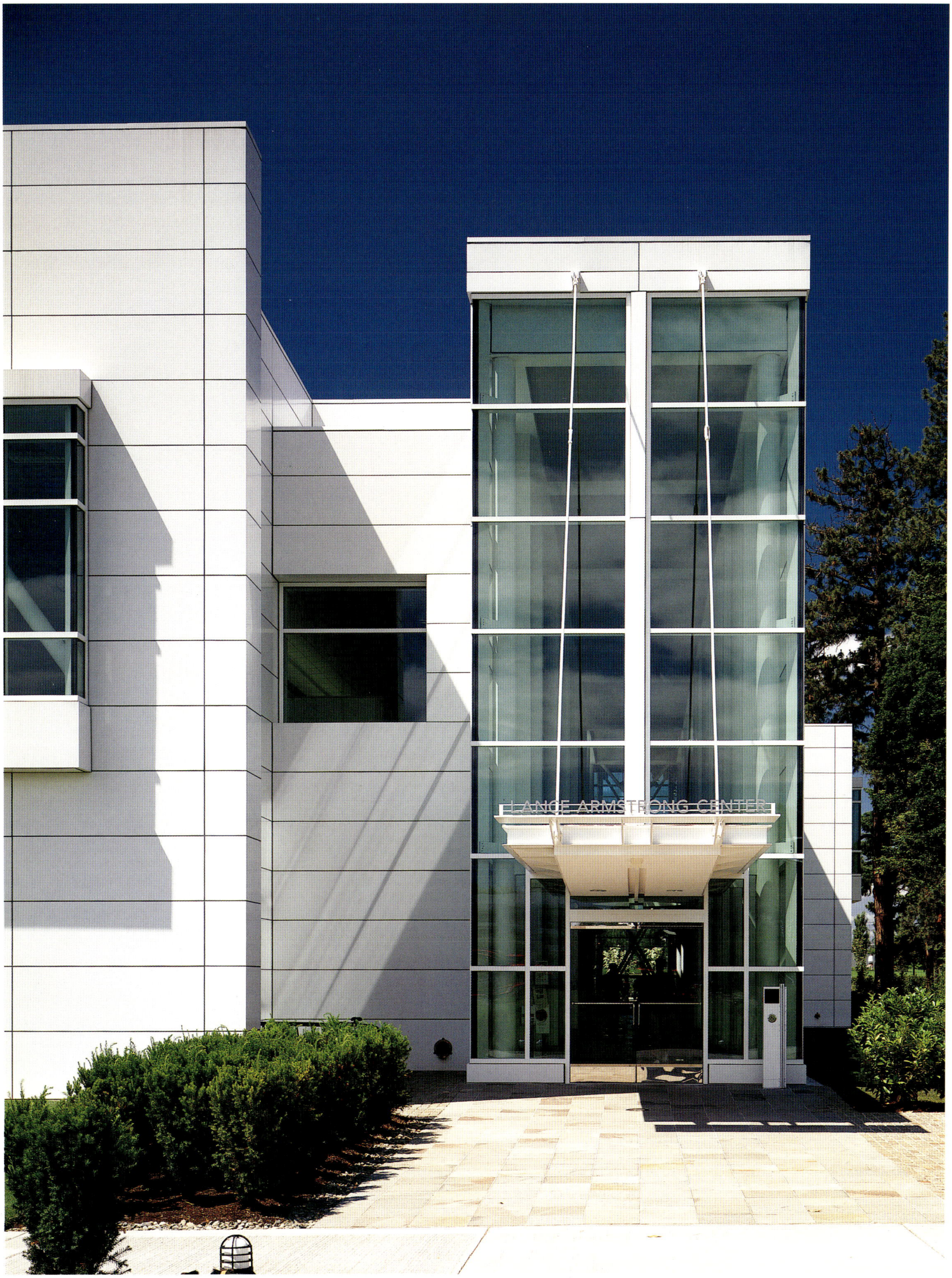

3

Lance Armstrong Recreation Center,
Nike World Campus
Beaverton, Oregon, USA
Thompson Vaivoda & Associates
Architects, Inc.

Opposite:
Rock-climbing and bouldering walls occupy southwest corner

5 Circulation spine/gallery joins lobby and outdoor spaces

6 Pool area opens to north light

7 Lobby is a three-dimensionally layered composition

Following pages:
Abundant glazing frames primary circuit and weight room

Photo credit: Strode Photographic

5

6

7

PRECOR

PRECOR

Sunken Gymnasium, Primary School Unterfeld
Lauterach, Austria
Elmar K. Ludescher, Architect

1 School wing and sunken gymnasium define sports area
2 School wing stands in contrast to transparency of sunken gymnasium
3 External entry to sunken gymnasium with view to courtyard
4 Sunken gymnasium with 'floating' roof allowing view to entire site

Photo credit: Bruno Klomfar

1

2

3

4

1

2

3

4

5

Olympic Velodrome
Bankstown, New South Wales, Australia
Ryder Associates Architects

1 Roof dome from northwest
2 Sunrise at Olympic Velodrome
3 Glazed foyer
4 Light diffuser—part of ESD program
5 Natural daylight and views out

Photo credit: Peter Hyatt

Olympic Velodrome
Bankstown, New South Wales, Australia
Ryder Associates Architects
6 Service pods with emergency exits
7 Main steel
8 Ove Arups' roof shell
9 Testing daylight system
Opposite:
Complementing curvatures
Photo credit: Peter Hyatt

7

6

8

9

1

2

3

4

Audrey J. Walton Stadium
University of Missouri
Columbia, Missouri, USA
Peckham & Wright Architects, Inc.

1. Track, soccer, and softball stadium complex
2. Track level at stadium complex
3. MU athletes on track

Photo credit: MU Publications and Alumni Communication

State Hockey Centre
Homebush Bay, New South Wales, Australia
Ancher Mortlock Woolley Architects

4. Western façade
5. Angled masts set lights in optimum position
6. Completely suspended roof
7. Concourse around pitch

Photo credit: Patrick Bingham-Hall

5

6

7

8

State Hockey Centre
Homebush Bay, New South Wales, Australia
Ancher Mortlock Woolley Architects
8 View of pitch from back of grandstand
Photo credit: Patrick Bingham-Hall

BIOGRAPHIES

Alfred Wong Partnership Pte Ltd

The firm of Alfred Wong Partnership Pte Ltd (AWP) was founded in 1957. The firm's philosophy is centered on providing a high standard of design and execution. Their track record includes educational buildings, hi-tech pharmaceutical plants, commercial projects, and special building types such as marinas. The next marina project designed by the firm will be located in west Malaysia.

To broaden the scope of their professional activities, AWP was incorporated into a private limited company in 1996.

Based in Singapore, the firm is active throughout Southeast Asia and China. AWP's first project in China dates from 1981 and presently work in the country's major cities is undertaken by a multidisciplinary team with links to associated Chinese design institutes. In addition to architectural services, this multidisciplinary team offers master planning and landscape design expertise.

AWP continues to be active in Malaysia, Indonesia and, more recently, Vietnam. The company is certified by ISO 9001 having first attained certification in 1997.

Alfred Wong Partnership Pte Ltd
Architects and Urban Designers
111 North Bridge Road
Singapore 179098
Tel: +65 6337 6777
Fax: +65 6339 6956
Email: awplc@awp.com.sg
Website: http://www.awp.com.sg

ARC/Architectural Resources Cambridge, Inc.

Founded in 1969, ARC/Architectural Resources Cambridge, Inc. is a fully integrated architectural design firm, providing services in the fields of architecture, planning, programming and interior design, including feasibility analyses, land-use planning, site design, master planning, programming, building design, construction documentation and administration, as well as space planning, furnishing and equipment selection.

The firm has designed athletic complexes for schools, colleges and universities. These projects have incorporated gymnasiums, fitness centers, indoor tracks, pools, ice rinks, squash, basketball and volleyball courts, and in one case, a 44,500-seat stadium, including support facilities. The firm has also designed boathouses for a number of independent and higher academic institutions.

ARC's higher education clients include Boston College, Boston University, Duke, Harvard, Princeton, Syracuse and Tufts, as well as state universities in Colorado, Iowa, Massachusetts and Missouri. In addition to the public elementary, middle and high schools designed by the firm. ARC has also provided services to many of the top eastern independent schools including Berkshire, Deerfield, Hotchkiss, Mercersburg, Milton Academy, St. George's, and St. Paul's. Clients in the corporate sector include Abbott Labs, Bayer Diagnostics, EMD Pharmaceuticals, Millapore, and Genzyme Corporation.

Based in Cambridge, Massachusetts, the firm has a staff of 60 professionals. Nationally recognized for excellence in architecture, ARC/Architectural Resources Cambridge, Inc. has received numerous awards from the American Institute of Architects and other professional organizations. Additional information can be found at www.arcusa.com.

ARC/Architectural Resources Cambridge, Inc.
140 Mount Auburn Street
Cambridge, Massachusetts 02138, USA
Tel: +1 617 547 0764
Fax: +1 617 547 2442
Email: arcmail@arcusa.com
Website: http://www.arcusa.com

Cannon Design

Founded over 50 years ago, Cannon Design is an internationally ranked multidisciplinary firm of 500, recognized for design excellence and technological innovation, and known for performance and dedication to client service. A 'single firm, multi-office' practice approach enables Cannon Design to focus staff resources to meet client needs through a network of 10 regional offices nationwide. By assembling all disciplines within the organization, a committed team of architects, engineers, planners and interior designers, offer clients a single point of responsibility and accountability, ensuring each project's success.

Cannon Design is focused upon developing long-term relationships with their clients based upon the trust earned through performance. The firm strives to create environments that are a thoughtful response to the program mission, physical setting and functional purpose, reflecting the spirit and personality of each owner.

Cannon Design has defined its mission clearly with a focus on quality—with client satisfaction as the ultimate measurement. As a leader in quality, Cannon Design works continuously to advance the state of the art, contributing to the built environment and quality of life of the people for whom the firm creates living and working spaces.

Cannon Design
2170 Whitehaven Road
Grand Island, New York 14072, USA
Tel: +1 716 773 6800
Fax: +1 716 773 5909
Email: chilliers@cannondesign.com
Website: http://www.cannondesign.com

Centerbrook Architects and Planners, LLC

Centerbrook is an architecture and planning firm that was established in 1975. Located in a renovated factory on the Falls River in the village of Centerbrook, Connecticut, the firm has five partners, two principals, and an overall staff of 80.

The firm designs architecture that is unique and uplifting, that fulfills program and budget, that enriches surrounding context, and that provides commodity and delight for inhabitants. Centerbrook buildings reflect exploration and response to client needs. Architectural writers have noted that the firm's work is innovative while varying from vernacular to modern according to the situation of its projects. Centerbrook has no over-arching style and prefers to explore unique solutions for each project.

The firm offers the following services: planning and urban design, feasibility studies, architectural programming, architectural design and sustainable design, interior design, furniture and fixture design, landscape design, project management, and assistance with fundraising.

The firm has received 222 awards for design excellence for a wide variety of work. Its institutional experience spans academic to civic buildings and includes art centers, museums, event centers, laboratories, offices, and religious buildings. The firm also designs private residences. In 1998, Centerbrook received the national AIA Firm Award, the highest honor the American Institute of Architects can confer on a firm.

Centerbrook has pioneered interactive techniques for bringing clients and users into the design process and enriching its architecture by their involvement.

Centerbrook's work has been the focus of 295 articles and books. These include two books published by the AIA Press, *Centerbrook: Reinventing American Architecture* by Michael Crosbie and *Centerbrook, Volume 2* by Andrea Oppenheimer Dean. A third book, titled *The Enthusiasms of Centerbrook*, written by the partners of the firm, was published in 2001, with an introduction by architecture critic John Morris Dixon.

Centerbrook Architects and Planners, LLC
67 Main Street
P.O. Box 955
Centerbrook, Connecticut 06409, USA
Tel: + 1 860 767 0175
Fax: + 1 860 767 8719
Email: last name@centerbrook.com
Website: http://www.centerbrook.com

Ellerbe Becket

High design value, high construction value and certainty of outcome—Ellerbe Becket has offered these benefits to clients for nearly 100 years. The firm's knowledge and creativity result in building designs of the highest quality and construction that delivers certainty of outcome. Projects are completed as planned, a trait that has fostered long-term relationships with clients as diverse as the Mayo Clinic, State Farm Mutual Automobile Insurance Company, Ryan Companies US Inc. and numerous federal agencies.

Ellerbe Becket's mission is:

Collaboration—an integrated team represents all aspects of design and construction, and involves clients from the start. Multiple locations give the firm the advantage of being able to work locally.

Creativity—Ellerbe Becket project teams work together from beginning to end, understanding the complexities of the design and construction process. They approach decision making and problem solving with ingenuity and imagination.

Innovation—inspired designs accommodate growth and change, and meet clients' business goals. By remaining apprised of its clients' industries the firm takes facility design one step further.

The Ellerbe Becket name is synonymous with outstanding hospitals and clinics, stadiums and arenas, heating and cooling systems, and mission critical facilities. But the firm's practice extends to higher education, development, interiors, and the government and corporate sectors. Ellerbe Becket demonstrates this expertise in buildings such as the Ronald Reagan Building and International Trade Center in Washington, D.C.; the Kingdom Centre in Riyadh, Saudi Arabia; Mayo Clinic in Rochester, Minneapolis; the Saitama Super Arena in Saitama, Japan; Southern Methodist University's Gerald J. Ford Stadium in Dallas, Texas; and E*TRADE's Regional Operations Center in Atlanta, Georgia.

The architecture, engineering and construction industry is changing constantly. Yesterday's impossibilities are today's standards. In this dynamic environment, Ellerbe Becket leads the way.

Ellerbe Becket
4600 Madison Avenue
Kansas City, Missouri 64112, USA
Tel: +1 816 561 4443
Fax: +1 816 561 2863
Email: margaret_stout@ellerbebecket.com
Website: http://www.ellerbebecket.com

Kuwabara Payne McKenna Blumberg Architects

Kuwabara Payne McKenna Blumberg Architects has developed an international reputation for excellence in architecture, urban design, and interior design. The four partners, Bruce Kuwabara, Thomas Payne, Marianne McKenna, and Shirley Blumberg are committed to developing and delivering physical environments that reinforce and express their clients' needs and objectives. The work of KPMB is complex and diverse in both scale and type. It has been recognized for its responsiveness to the urban context as acts and interventions of city building, as well as for its careful, rigorous attention to detailing and technical execution.

The firm has won seven Governor General's Awards for Architecture: Woodsworth College at the University of Toronto; King James Palace, Toronto; Kitchener City Hall, Kitchener; the Reisman-Jenkinson Studio/Residence, Richmond Hill; the Design Exchange, Toronto; Grand Valley Institution for Women, Kitchener; and the Joseph S. Stauffer Library, Queen's University, Kingston. KPMB recently won a national competition for the design of the new Canadian Embassy in Berlin, in association with Architects Gagnon, Lettellier, Cyr and Smith Carter Architects & Engineers Inc.

The office has 11 associates, and a total staff of approximately 55. The members of the firm believe in the value of working on interdisciplinary teams with proficient consultants. They practise architecture at the highest level, and are focused on bringing the work to completion on time and on budget. The studio atmosphere of the office creates a stimulating creative work environment that fosters complementarity and collaboration.

The boundaries between project types of the firm are less critical than the intensity and rigor of design and execution at every scale of the work. If one were to look for a common idea and expression in the work by the firm, it may be claimed that it is a contemporary urbanity and high level of quality and craftsmanship.

Kuwabara Payne McKenna Blumberg Architects
322 King Street West, 3rd Floor
Toronto, Ontario, M5V 1J2, Canada
Tel: + 1 416 977 5104
Fax: +1 416 598 9840
Email: kpmb@kpmbarchitects.com
Website: http://www.kpmb.com

Michael Graves & Associates

Since founding his practice in 1964 in Princeton, New Jersey, Michael Graves has been a leader in architectural design. His body of work in the US alone includes the Humana Building, projects for Disney, the Denver Central Library, and the National Collegiate Athletic Association (NCAA) Headquarters and Hall of Champions. These buildings, along with many other significant projects all over the world such as the Headquarters for the Ministry of Health and Sport in The Hague, The Netherlands, have directly influenced the transformation of urban architecture from abstract modernism toward more contextual and traditional themes.

The architectural practice encompasses a wide variety of building types, including: large-scale mixed-use projects; office buildings and corporate headquarters; university buildings of various types; civic institutions such as courthouses and municipal buildings; educational and cultural facilities such as public libraries, museums, and theaters; hotels and resorts; facilities for sports, entertainment and retail enterprises; healthcare facilities; apartment buildings, and single-family residences. Graves is also well known for his design of furniture, furnishings, and artifacts.

A native of Indianapolis, Graves received his architectural training at the University of Cincinnati and Harvard University. In 1960, he won the Rome Prize and studied at The American Academy in Rome, of which he is now a trustee. Graves began teaching at Princeton University in 1962 and is now Robert Schirmer Professor of Architecture, Emeritus, after having taught architecture there for almost 40 years. His firm, Michael Graves & Associates, currently comprises 100 people.

Michael Graves is a Fellow of the American Institute of Architects (AIA). He has received over 140 awards for his professional achievements, including the 1999 National Medal of Arts (a Presidential award); the 2001 AIA Gold Medal, the Institute's highest individual honor; and the 2001 $50,000 Frank Annunzio Award from the Christopher Columbus Fellowship Foundation.

Michael Graves & Associates
341 Nassau Street
Princeton, New Jersey 08540, USA
Tel: +1 609 924 6409
Fax: +1 609 924 1795
Email: info@michaelgraves.com
Website: http://www.michaelgraves.com

P&T Group

The P&T Group, formerly known as Palmer and Turner Hong Kong, is the oldest and largest international architectural and engineering practice in Southeast Asia. With over 550 staff, working from offices located in Hong Kong, Macau, Bangkok, Malaysia, Taiwan, Singapore and Shanghai, projects are also undertaken in most other Southeast Asian countries.

First established in Hong Kong around 1868, P&T since its inception has proved to be a major contributor to the physical development of the region, responsible for many of its old and new architectural landmarks.

The P&T Group offers the full range of architectural, engineering and planning services, with full support from in-house interior and graphic design divisions. Model-making, extensive computer facilities and full administrative support complete the service of total design.

The group is committed to the pursuit of excellence in the architectural and engineering fields and aims to improve people's quality of life by contributing to the design of the physical environment. Professional emphasis is placed on visual and functional elements of design, to create buildings that are both aesthetically pleasing and sympathetic to their environment.

The group's growth is a reflection of the increasing number of large-scale projects demanding the creativity and expertise of many professional services to clients. The number of design awards received over the years demonstrates P&T's success in this.

P&T Group
25/F OTB Building
160 Gloucester Road
Hong Kong, SAR, PRC
Tel: +852 2575 6575
Fax: +852 2891 3834
Email: ptaehk@p-t-group.com
Website: http://www.p-t-group.com

Richard Dattner & Partners Architects PC

Richard Dattner & Partners Architects is a 60-person firm based in New York City with a wide range of corporate, institutional and public agency clients. Established by founding partner Richard Dattner FAIA in 1964, with present partners Joseph Coppola AIA, William Stein AIA, Bernard Zipprich AIA and Beth Greenberg AIA, the firm has a strong specialty in sports and recreation facilities. In addition to the projects illustrated in this volume, recent examples include:

- The Pottruck Health and Fitness Center at the University of Pennsylvania
- For the NYC 2012 Olympic Bid, the Boxing and Rhythmic Gymnastics Venue at the 369th Armory in Harlem, and the Field Hockey Venue at Columbia University's Wien Stadium—formerly designed by Richard Dattner & Partners Architects
- Hudson River Park, Segments 6 and 7—from West 26th to West 59th Streets in Manhattan
- The Senator Lavalle Stadium at the State University of New York at Stony Brook
- The McBurney YMCA, and the Harlem YMCA in Manhattan
- The Berkeley-Carroll School Swimming Pool and Gymnasium
- The New York Athletic Club Swimming Pool and Locker Facility.

Richard Dattner & Partners has a long-standing commitment to sustainable design—with sensitivity to energy efficiency, benign construction materials, a healthy indoor environment, and respect for the surrounding communities in which their projects are located. The firm balances its clients' aspirations with close attention to available resources and life-cycle savings to produce projects, which have received over 100 design awards.

Richard Dattner & Partners Architects PC
130 West 57th Street, Suite 3C
New York, New York 10019, USA
Tel: +1 212 247 2660
Fax: +1 212 245 7132
Email: info@dattner.com
Website: http://www.dattner.com

Ryder Associates Architects

Initially, Paul Ryder took an apprenticeship diploma in aircraft engineering in preparation for a career at Qantas Airways in Australia. He became one of the youngest engineers in that company qualified to certify Boeing engines and airframes. In 1980 he obtained his Bachelor Degree in Architecture at the University of New South Wales in Sydney.

Prior to setting up Ryder Associates Architects he spent several years in Europe, employed as an architect in London where he worked on a number of significant UK projects. Back in Australia, the small team competed in several architectural competitions with some success. Notably the firm won the Sydney Olympic Velodrome project in competition in the early 1990s. That project is illustrated in this volume. The firm continues to enter competitions today, having won, been commended and selected as finalists in major competitions in Australia and overseas.

Ryder Associates remains a small team of architects and designers taking on a variety of design briefs that include private houses and mixed residential and commercial projects along with a strong core in sports and public architecture. The firm always aspires to produce creative, original and innovative design solutions—recognizing that this creates lasting value in buildings.

The work is informed by the continuous development of Environmental Sustainability in buildings, having achieved substantial implementations of ESD in every project. It is further recognized for its innovative solutions with a range of construction technologies including the reappraisal of many traditional building systems and their use in new ways.

Ryder Associates Architects
414 Edgecliff Road, Woollahra
Sydney, NSW 2025
Australia
Ph: +61 2 9331 4479
Fax: +61 2 9360 1021
Email: info@ryders.com.au
Website: http://www.ryders.com.au

SmithGroup JJR

SmithGroup JJR's diversified practice includes a professional staff of over 140 landscape architects, urban and regional planners, civil engineers and environmental scientists. The firm coordinates multidisciplinary services to provide clients with seamless idea-driven solutions. The firm's projects encompass cities and communities, settings for learning and healthcare, waterfronts, property development, water resources, recreation and transportation. SmithGroup JJR's results enhance the quality of the physical environment and contribute to people's enjoyment of the places where they live, work and play.

The firm's designs succeed because they satisfy the client's aspirations, the interests of the users and the natural systems that underlie the dynamics of each recreational space. From the planning of local or regional open space systems and large-scale ecological restoration programs to master planning and implementation of local, regional, state and national parks, trail systems, golf courses, athletic facilities and stadiums—SmithGroup JJR's reputation speaks for the success of this philosophy.

Representative projects include:

- Athletic Facilities—Northwestern University, Evanston, Illinois
- State Park—Milwaukee Lakeshore State Park, Milwaukee, Wisconsin
- Parks and Recreation Master Plan—City of Elgin, Elgin, Illinois
- Urban Park—Seward Park, Chicago, Illinois
- Park Master Plan—Carmel Central Park Master Plan, Carmel, Indiana
- Nature Center—Crosswinds Marsh Interpretive Preserve, Sumpter Township, Michigan
- Golf Course—Tournament Players Club of Michigan, Dearborn, Michigan
- Municipal Park—South Lakefront Framework Plan, Chicago, Illinois.

SmithGroup JJR
30 W. Monroe, Suite 1010
Chicago, Illinois 60603, USA
Tel: +1 312 641 0770
Fax: +1 312 641 6728
Email: info@smithgroup.com
Website: http://www.smithgroupjjr.com

Theo. David Architects

The design process of Theo. David Architects is meant to produce innovative concepts which provide a dynamic identity for its diverse clients, while responding to programmatic needs in the most imaginative way possible. The process includes client–user input during all phases of programming and design development.

The practice is headed by Theoharis David FAIA who is also Professor of Architecture at Pratt Institute in New York. It has acquired extensive experience in the United States and abroad, and its architecture has received design awards at city, state, national and international levels.

In the United States, built projects include medical facilities, private residences, churches, corporate interiors, retail space design and the restoration of historical buildings, in addition to low- and medium-rise urban housing.

Internationally, Theo. David Architects is affiliated with Kal Engineering, civil and structural engineers, with head offices in Nicosia, Cyprus. This in-house technological support provides an extensive range of structural and infrastructure engineering services, on-site inspection, quality control and contract administration.

Theo. David Architects and KAL Engineering have designed in Cyprus, the Middle East and Greece, corporate and educational facilities, public schools, civic structures, athletic stadiums and arenas, industrial structures and residential neighborhoods. They have also generated comprehensive master plans for large housing and tourism developments.

Theo. David Architects TDA/KAL
170 Duane Street
New York, New York 10013, USA
Tel: +1 212 226 0788
Fax: +1 212 226 7724
Email: tdanyc@aol.com
Website: http://www.NewYork-Architects.com/TDANYC

Thompson Vaivoda & Associates Architects, Inc.

Thompson Vaivoda & Associates Architects, Inc. (TVA) is a full service architecture, planning and interiors firm founded in 1984 and headquartered in Portland, Oregon, USA. The firm has gained a reputation throughout the United States for exceptional design and planning solutions to a wide variety of building and project types, winning nearly 50 design and construction awards at international as well as local levels.

In an ever-increasing world of specialists, the firm has made a conscious and deliberate effort to remain generalists. TVA believes that design is an attitude, a frame of mind, a way of looking at the world, and a method for ordering decisions more than it is an activity learned by mere repetition. Time and again lessons learned in one arena can be applied in another.

Sporting spaces and recreational venues have long been a mainstay of the firm's work. The Bo Jackson and Lance Armstrong (illustrated above) Buildings on the Nike, Inc. Beaverton, Oregon corporate campuses are premier examples of the firm's work, joining design, program and construction excellence in facilities that nurture community.

The urge to build community is as fundamental to the human condition as food, clothing and shelter. The social aspects of our existence are often manifest in buildings and places that support and celebrate a common purpose. Buildings for education, worship, healing and recreation all nurture in part our basic instinct for community. Structures and spaces can be uplifting and nurturing. The manipulation of natural light is a powerful tool available to the design team from both the aesthetic and sustainability perspectives.

Recreational activities and the spaces they require provide unique opportunities to achieve multiple objectives while imparting a lasting impression on those who use the facility.

Thompson Vaivoda & Associates Architects, Inc.
920 S.W. Sixth Avenue
Portland, Oregon 97204, USA
Tel: +1 503 220 0668
Fax: +1 503 225 0803
Email: tva@tvapdx.com
Website: http://www.tvapdx.com

INDEX